CONTENTS

Early days	2
Amy spreads her wings	4
Jason and the big adventure	6
Problems and progress	8
Flight into fame	10
Back home: Amy the heroine	12
Amy and Jim	14
Solo and duet	16
The final record	18
Flying for a living	20
Amy's last flight	22
Index	24

Early days

Amy Johnson was born on July 1, 1903, in Hull — a busy fishing town in the north of England. Her father Will was a fish merchant, her mother Ciss the chapel organist, and she had two younger sisters.

No one could have predicted Amy's future fame from her quiet early life. As a young child, her exploits were limited to such things as setting out by herself on a bus "to the north" with just a few pennies from her piggy-bank.

But as Amy grew up, her more adventurous spirit began to show. During the First World War, when Amy was eleven years old, she would run out to watch the Zeppelin raids until her father chased her indoors. And at school her favorite activities were sports such as hockey, gymnastics, and cricket, which were considered more suitable for boys. In one cricket match, a ball broke both her front teeth; it made her feel shy about smiling for a long time.

She also loved going to "the pictures" — the silent movies of the time greatly appealed to Amy's imagination.

LEON
ERROL
IN

PIRATE

SILENT SCREEN

Amy spreads her wings

Amy did well at school and went on to study at Sheffield University. She planned to become a teacher, but instead moved to London and worked as a secretary.

In the 1920s, light airplanes were very popular with the general public. There were races, aerobatic contests and pioneering flights across continents and oceans. Amy joined the London Aeroplane Club and began taking lessons. She was twenty-five years old.

Amy and the Cirrus Moth biplane in which she learned to fly.

After fifteen hours of instruction, Amy flew solo for the first time on June 9, 1929. That night she wrote to her mother, "I am very excited tonight, as I have just successfully accomplished a first solo at the airport."

Amy wanted to know more about airplane engines, and started working in the club hangars during her vacations. At first the male engineers would have nothing to do with her, but she persisted, and became a qualified engineer. Amy passed her "A" Class Flying License, and decided to make flying her career.

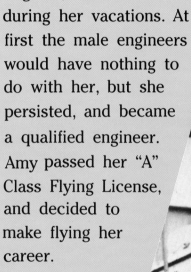

Amy passed her airplane engineers' examination in December 1929. She was the first female ground engineer in England.

Jason and the big adventure

Amy was told that a woman pilot would have to fly from England to Australia to prove that she was the equal of a man. She decided to take up the challenge! Bert Hinkler had set the record for the 10,000 mile distance only the year before, and Amy wanted to beat his time of fifteen and a half days.

She raised enough money to buy a Gypsy Moth biplane, which she named *Jason*.

Jason: Amy had *Jason* painted green, her lucky color. Jason had a wooden frame covered with fabric, and its wings were held together with wire rigging.

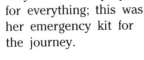

Amy had to be prepared for everything; this was her emergency kit for the journey.

Amy left from Croydon, England, on May 5, 1930, and the first stage went smoothly. At dawn on the fourth day she took off for Baghdad, flying nearly five hundred miles across the desert.

In Baghdad, Amy first took to wearing shorts as the most comfortable flying kit for hot countries. At the time, it was very rare to see a woman wearing shorts.

Amy had almost reached Baghdad when she was caught up in a violent sandstorm. The engine stopped and Amy made an almost miraculous engine-off landing in the desert. She had to hang on to *Jason* for two hours to stop it from being blown over and wrecked. As the storm raged, Amy clutched her revolver against the wild dogs that were barking in the distance. When the storm died down, Amy and the little Moth flew on to Baghdad.

Problems and progress

News of Amy's flight was attracting a lot of attention in England, and by the time she reached Karachi, Amy was a celebrity; she was two days ahead of Hinkler's schedule!

On her way to Allahabad, Amy ran out of fuel and had to land between trees and buildings at Jhansi. One of *Jason*'s wings was broken and had to be repaired before Amy could continue on to Calcutta.

Then, when she was flying to Rangoon, Amy faced the terror of a monsoon. She was blinded by the heavy rain, and *Jason* was damaged on landing.

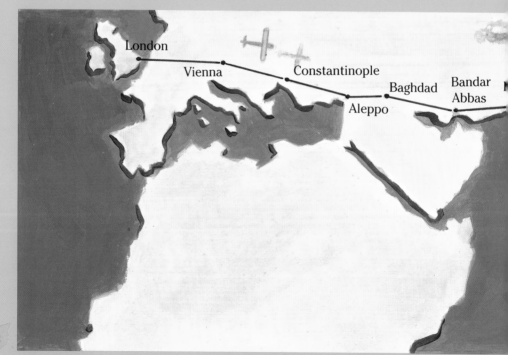

The teachers and pupils from a school helped Amy with repairs, and twenty men's shirts were sewn together to cover the wing!

Amy had now lost her lead over Hinkler, but she was determined to go on. She was now flying over vast stretches of ocean and jungle which had barely been mapped. There was little hope of rescue if things went wrong.

From Singapore she cabled to her father, "Cannot break record, weather dreadful ..." Her parents cabled back, "You are wonderful. Nobody worrying about record."

Flight into fame

Amy flew into monsoons and buffeting winds again on the way to Sourabaya in the Dutch East Indies; she was lost and unable to see when the sun shone through a gap in the clouds and a rainbow showed her the way. She landed on Java, and the next day she reached Sourabaya.

She then flew to Atamboea on the island of Timor, and on to Darwin. But Amy didn't arrive in Darwin as expected — she seemed to have vanished. Then the news came through that Amy was safe; she had run low on fuel and landed on a tiny island. On Saturday, May 24, she flew across 500 miles of water to Australia, and into fame. Amy had taken nineteen days to fly 10,000 miles in a small single-engined aircraft with an open cockpit. She had earned a permanent place in history as one of aviation's great pioneers.

There were over eight hundred telegrams of congratulation waiting for Amy in Darwin. She spent six weeks touring Australia and attending dinners and banquets held in her honor. Amy found the demands of the huge crowds tiring after the tension and adventure of her long flight.

Back home: Amy the heroine

Amy had originally planned to fly back to England, but she was so exhausted when she reached Australia that she decided to return by ship instead. By now she was famous all over the world.

When she arrived back in London, more than a million people were waiting for her. Later, Amy was presented with a gold cup, and her fans gave her a new airplane, *Jason II*.

The streets of London were lined with cheering fans eager to catch a glimpse of Amy.

Amy was presented with a car in honor of her flight —
it even had a model of *Jason* on the hood!

Amy and Jim

A my had a short vacation before starting on her next adventure — a solo flight from London to China. She set off on New Year's Day, 1931, but became lost in heavy fog and had to make a forced landing near Warsaw, Poland.

In July, 1931, Amy again tried to fly to the "Far East," and this time she was successful, arriving in Tokyo on August 6.

Amy with her co-pilot, Jack Humphreys, and *Jason II* after their flight to Japan.

But this time Amy's flight didn't make the headlines; the newspapers were full of the story of an Australian pilot who had beaten Hinkler's record and reached England in nine days — Jim Mollison.

Jim and Amy inspecting Jim's plane, *The Heart's Content*, before Jim's solo flight from England to South America.

Jim Mollison was also a pioneer aviator. He and Amy met after he had made the first light-plane flight across the Sahara desert to Cape Town. They became engaged and were married in July, 1932. They had their honeymoon in Scotland — and even flew there in separate planes!

Soon after this, Jim successfully flew solo over the Atlantic Ocean from Ireland to Newfoundland, Canada. Both Amy and Jim were in the headlines; the marriage of two well-known aviators had captured the attention of their many fans.

Solo and duet

A my's next solo flight was from London to Cape Town. Just as a "sporting effort" she wanted to beat Jim's record of four days and seventeen hours. Amy's flight in *The Desert Cloud* cut ten hours from Jim's record. She then flew back to London, setting a record for the round trip.

Amy arrived from Cape Town on December 18 1932, and was again greeted by admiring crowds.
Her double-flight in record time brought her a new wave of popularity.

The "Flying Sweethearts," as Amy and Jim were called, made plans for a record-breaking, long-distance flight. They would cross the Atlantic to New York, then set off for Baghdad, then fly back to London. Their new plane was the *Seafarer*, a twin-engined de Havilland Dragon.

The *Seafarer* in flight.
The *Seafarer* was painted black,
Jim's favorite color.

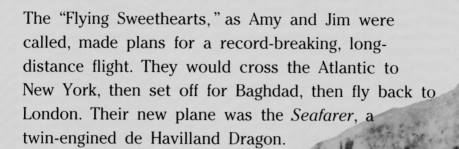

The *Seafarer* was heavily loaded with fuel, and crashed on take-off. Although Amy and Jim weren't hurt, the flight was delayed for a month. They made a second attempt on July 22, 1933, taking less fuel. This was a mistake; they ran out of fuel and crash-landed at Bridgeport, fifty miles short of New York.

The final record

After Amy and Jim recovered from their injuries, Amy stayed on in the United States for seven months. She became friends with the famous American aviator, Amelia Earhart. Amy was very popular with the American crowds, and Jim became jealous of all the attention they gave her.

Amy and Jim started in the 1934 England-Australia Air Race. They halved the non-stop record from London to Karachi, but were then forced out of the race by engine failure.

Amy was in the news again in 1936 when she flew from London to Cape Town. She broke the latest London to Cape Town record, and also set records for the return flight and the round trip. Once again, the public responded to her courage and persistence. It was her last record attempt.

In late 1936, and after many disagreements, Amy and Jim finally agreed to divorce.

Crowds gathered at Croydon to welcome Amy when she arrived on the last lap of her flight from Cape Town. Jim is standing behind her. For her last record, Amy flew a Percival Gull, with long-range tanks and an enclosed cabin.

Flying for a living

I n 1937, Amy moved to the countryside. She had stopped making record-breaking flights, but she still led an adventurous life, taking up gliding and auto racing.

Amy wanted to continue flying, preferably in a way that would allow her to earn a living. But for a long time it seemed that, despite all of her experience, nobody was willing to hire a woman pilot.

Finally, in June 1939, she was offered a flying job with a small aviation company, and was at last earning her living as a commercial pilot.

A few months later, the outbreak of the Second World War brought an end to her job. Amy decided to join the Air Transport Auxiliary, or ATA, as it was more commonly known.

The ATA's job was to fly aircraft to where they were needed for war work, and to carry important people around the country. ATA pilots were not involved in combat, but they flew military aircraft without radios to keep in contact with base, and they were often pounced upon by enemy fighters.

Women pilots of the ATA. Amy's pioneering flights had helped women pilots to be taken seriously by their male colleagues. In the ATA, Amy fought for equal pay for equal work.

Jim Mollison had also joined the ATA, and he and Amy became good friends again. Women pilots in the ATA were paid much less than the men. Amy wrote to her father: "We ought to have the same when we're doing precisely the same job, don't you agree?" Later in the war, the male and female pilots of the ATA did receive equal pay.

Amy's last flight

T his was how the world read of Amy's disappearance. Amy had been on ATA duty, piloting an Airspeed Oxford, when she crashed into the Thames Estuary on January 5, 1941. She was never seen again.

The trawler HMS *Haslemere* was near the crash, and its commanding officer, Commander Walter Fletcher, dived overboard in a vain rescue attempt. The waters of the estuary were extremely cold, and Fletcher died later as a result of his efforts.

Why did Amy crash? No one is really sure. One suggestion is that she lost her way in bad weather and ran out of fuel after flying around for several hours. Amy knew the weather was bad before she took off on her last flight, but she had intended to fly above the clouds. "All right," she said, "I am going over the top." These were her last words, a fitting memorial to the courage and determination of a great aviator.

Index

"A" Class Flying License 5
Air Transport Auxiliary (ATA) 20-21
Airspeed Oxford 22
arriving in Australia 11

Baghdad 7

childhood 2
Cirrus Moth 4

dangers and difficulties 7, 8, 9, 10, 14, 17, 18, 21, 22
death 22
Desert Cloud 16
divorce 19
Dragon 17

Earhart, Amelia 18
England to Australia 6-11
England to Cape Town (1932) 16
England to Cape Town (1936) 19
England to China 14
England to New York 17
England to Tokyo 14
England–Australia Air Race 19
equal pay 21

fame and applause 8, 12-13, 16, 18, 19
first solo flight 5
First World War 2

ground engineering 5
Gypsy Moth 6

Heart's Content 15
Hinkler, Bert 6

Jason 6, 7, 8-9, 13
Jason II 14

Karachi 8

learning to fly 4-5
London Aeroplane Club 4

marriage 15
Mollison, Jim 14, 15, 17, 18, 19, 21
monsoons 8, 10

Percival Gull 19

Rangoon 8

school 2, 3
Seafarer 17
Second World War 20, 21
solo flights 7-11, 14, 16, 19

United States 18
university 4

women and flying 5, 6, 11, 20, 21, 22